THE WORSHIP PIANO METHOD

Songbook

LEVEL 2

To access audio visit:
www.halleonard.com/mylibrary

Enter Code
2913-8813-7856-1134

ISBN 978-1-4803-9458-2

HAL•LEONARD®
CORPORATION

7777 W. BLUEMOUND RD. P.O. BOX 13819 MILWAUKEE, WI 53213

Scripture taken from the New Century Version®
Copyright © 2005 by Thomas Nelson, Inc.
Used by permission. All rights reserved.

Visit Hal Leonard Online at
www.halleonard.com

Sing to the King

Words and Music by
Billy James Foote

Joyfully ♩ = 132

Come, let us sing a song, a song de - clar - ing we be - long to

Je - sus and He is all we need.

Lift up a song of praise, sing now with voic - es raised to

Je - sus. Sing to the King.

Thy Word
(Psalm 119:105)

Words and Music by Michael W. Smith
and Amy Grant

With confidence ♩ = 144

Thy Word is a lamp un-to my feet and a

light un - to my path.

Thy Word is a lamp un-to my feet and a

light un - to my path. _____

Forever Reign

Words and Music by Reuben Morgan
and Jason Ingram

With confidence ♩ = 168

Oh, I'm run - ning to Your arms, I'm run - ning to Your

arms. The rich - es of Your love will al - ways be e -

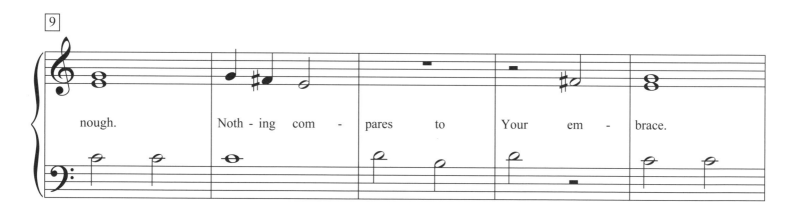

nough. Noth - ing com - pares to Your em - brace.

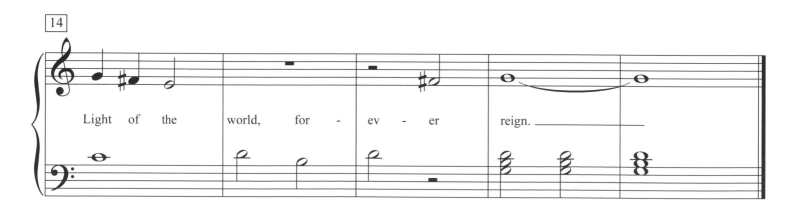

Light of the world, for - ev - er reign. _____

Take Me In

(Based on Isaiah 6:6–8)

Words and Music by
Dave Browning

Prayerfully ♩ = 138

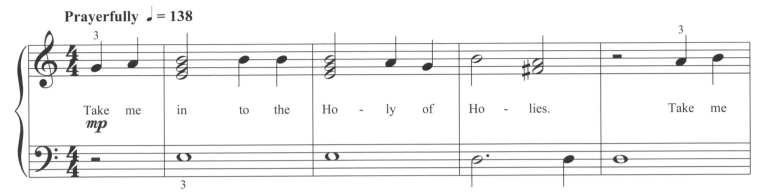

Take me in to the Ho - ly of Ho - lies. Take me

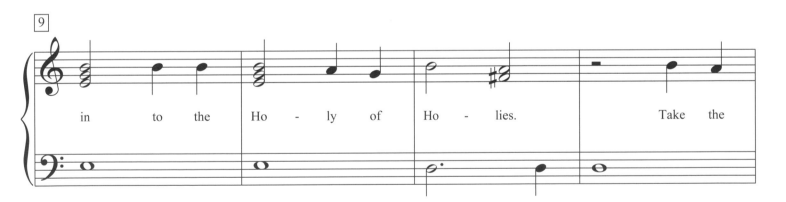

in by the blood of the Lamb. Take me

in to the Ho - ly of Ho - lies. Take the

coal, cleanse my lips, here I am.

I Will Follow

Words and Music by Chris Tomlin,
Reuben Morgan and Jason Ingram

Moderately fast ♩ = 100

We Will Glorify

Words and Music by
Twila Paris

Worshipfully ♩ = 80

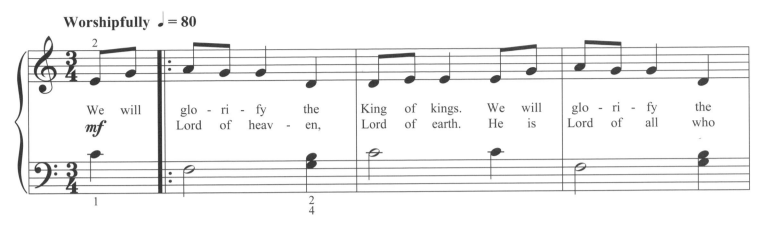

We will glo-ri-fy the King of kings. We will glo-ri-fy the
Lord of heav-en, Lord of earth. He is Lord of all who

Lamb. We will glo-ri-fy the Lord of lords, who ____
live. He is Lord a-bove the u-ni-verse. All ____

is the Great I AM. He is
praise to Him we

1. give.
2.

"Glorify the Lord with me, and let us praise His name together."
– Psalm 34:3, NCV®

Mighty Is Our God

Words and Music by Eugene Greco,
Gerrit Gustafson and Don Moen

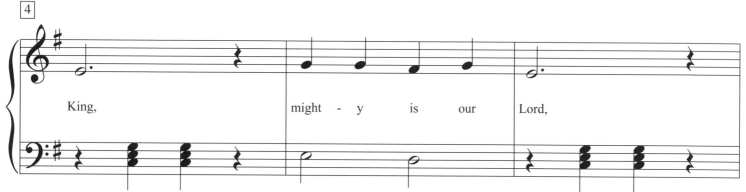

glo - ry to our Lord, Rul - er of ev - 'ry -

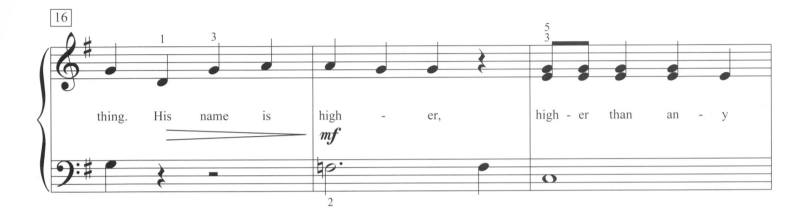

thing. His name is high - er, high - er than an - y

oth - er name. His pow'r is great - er, for

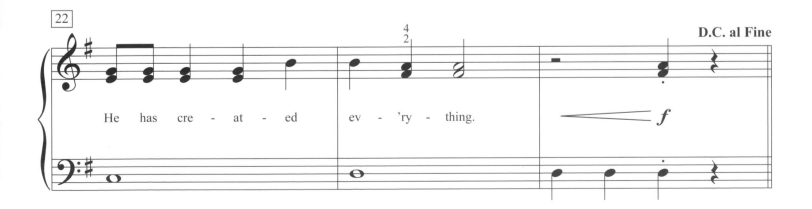

D.C. al Fine

He has cre - at - ed ev - 'ry - thing.

I Give You My Heart

Words and Music by
Reuben Morgan

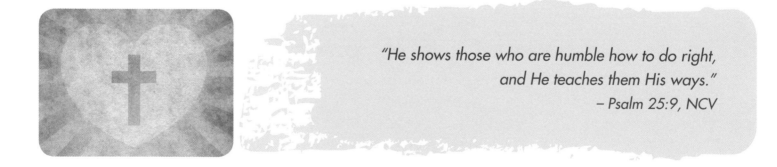

"He shows those who are humble how to do right, and He teaches them His ways."
– Psalm 25:9, NCV

Worthy, You Are Worthy

Words and Music by
Don Moen

Worshipfully ♩ = 80

Wor - thy, You are wor - thy. King of kings, Lord of lords, You are
Ho - ly, You are ho - ly. King of kings, Lord of lords, You are

wor - thy. Wor - thy, You are wor - thy. King of
ho - ly. Ho - ly, You are ho - ly. King of

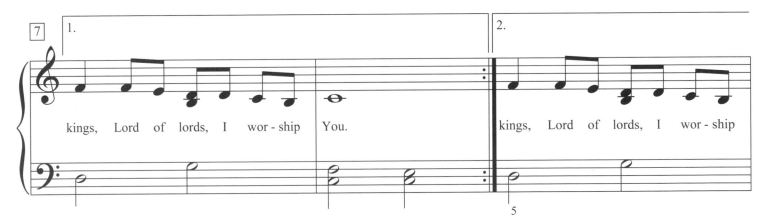

1.
kings, Lord of lords, I wor - ship You.

2.
kings, Lord of lords, I wor - ship

You. King of kings, Lord of lords, I wor - ship You.

The Stand

Words and Music by
Joel Houston

Steadily ♩ = 84

mf I'll stand with arms high and heart a-ban-doned, in awe of the

One who gave it all. I'll stand, my soul now to You sur-ren-dered.

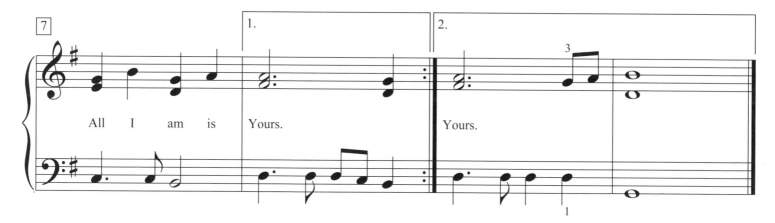

All I am is Yours. | 1. Yours. | 2. Yours.

"I will praise You as long as I live.
I will lift up my hands in prayer to Your name."
— Psalm 63:4, NCV

Whom Shall I Fear

(God of Angel Armies)

Words and Music by Chris Tomlin,
Ed Cash and Scott Cash

With confidence ♩ = 76

Come, Now Is the Time to Worship

Words and Music by
Brian Doerksen

To Coda

17

Come.

One day ev - 'ry tongue will con -

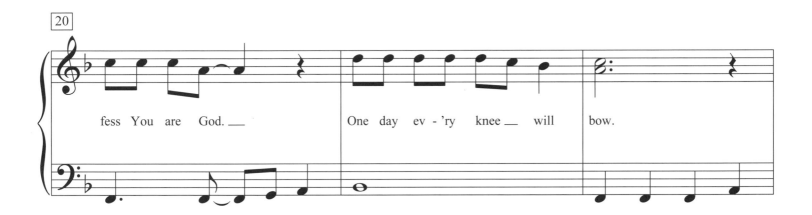

20

fess You are God. ___

One day ev - 'ry knee ___ will bow.

23

Still, the great - est treas - ure re - mains for those who glad - ly choose You

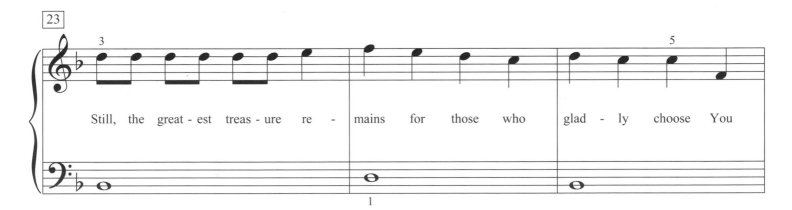

26

now.

D.C. al Coda

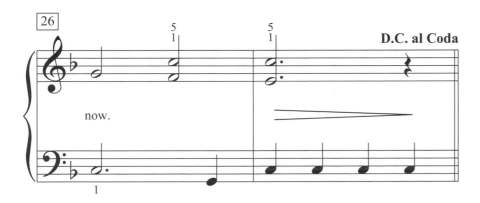

CODA

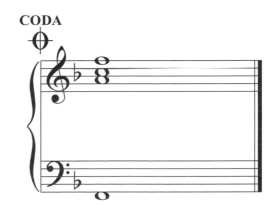